FACE PAINTING GO!

BOOK 1: BEGINNER DESIGNS

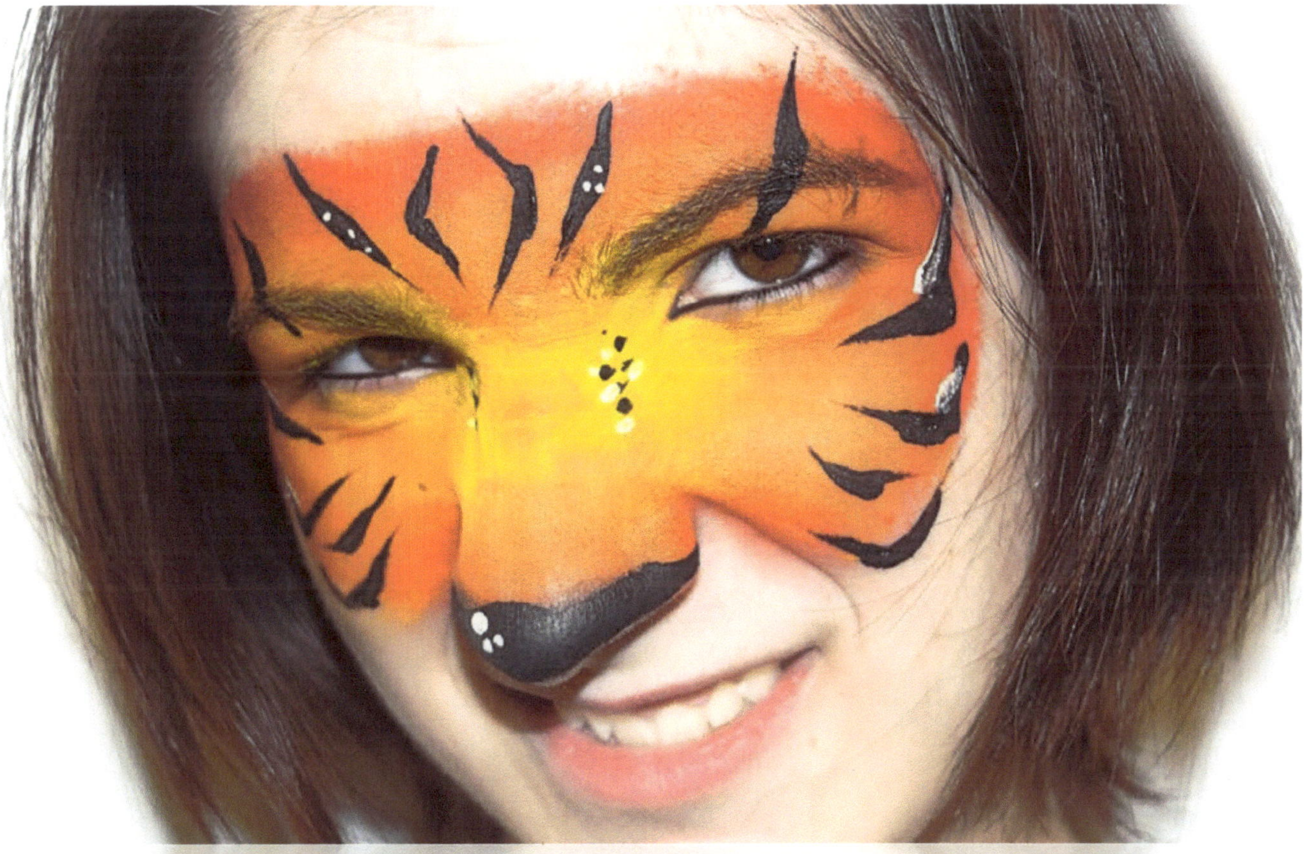

CHRISTEN HARRIS

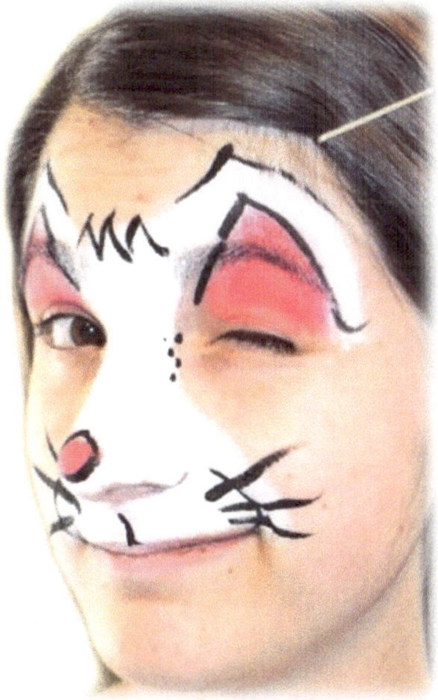

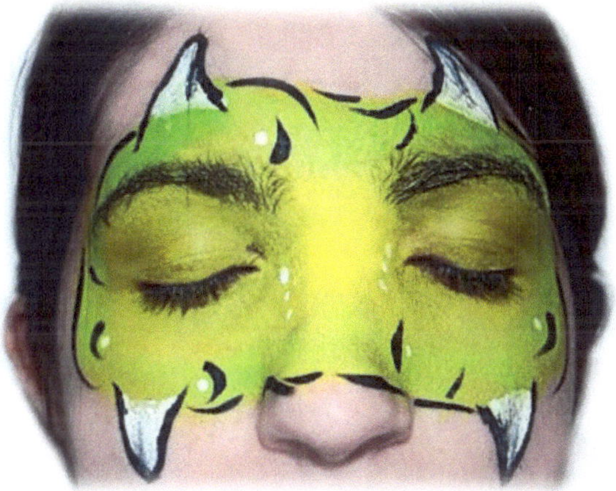

ISBN-13:
978-1530117130
ISBN-10:
1530117135

FOR AUBRI AND DAISY,
MY FAVORITE FACES.

SPECIAL THANKS TO

Aubrianna Harris

FOR MEGA-AWESOME MODELING.

HEALTH AND SAFETY

WHEN FACE PAINTING, SAFETY SHOULD BE YOUR #1 CONCERN.

*NEVER USE ANY SUPPLIES THAT WERE NOT MADE FOR FACE PAINTING. This includes paint, sponges, glitter, etc.

*ALWAYS WASH HANDS AND KEEP THEN CLEAN THOUGH THE ENTIRE PROCESS.

*WHEN WORKING FOR A GROUP, NEVER PAINT ANY CHOLD THAT HAS A SIGN OF ILLNESS. PAINT, BRUSHES, AND SPONGES CAN EASILY SPREAD GERMS NOT ONLY TO YOU, BUT TO OTHER CHILDREN.

*AFTER A PAINTING SESSION, ALL BRISHES AND SPONGES SHOULD BE CLEANED WITH ANTIBACTERAIL BRUSH CLEANER OR RUBBING ALCOHOL AND RINSED THUROUGHLY.

SUPPLIES

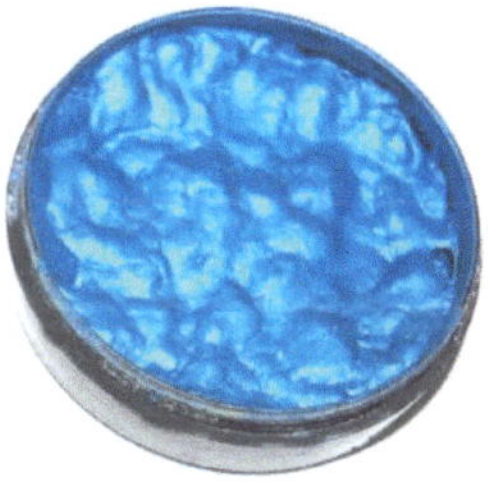

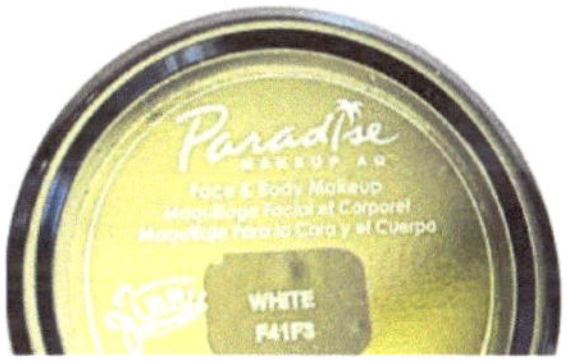

PAINT-

ALL PAINT SHOULD BE HYPOALLERGENIC AND MADE ONLY FOR THE PURPOSE OF FACE PAINTING. MY FAVORITES ARE 'MEHRON' AND 'PARADISE' CAKES.

SPONGES-

USE A HIGH DENSITY SPONGE FOR BEST COVERAGE.

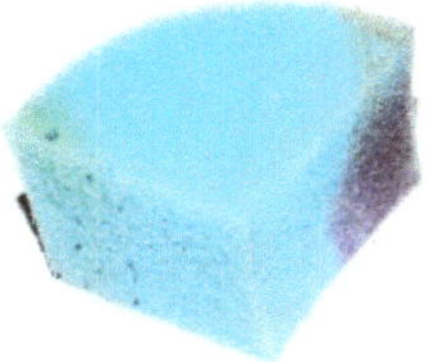

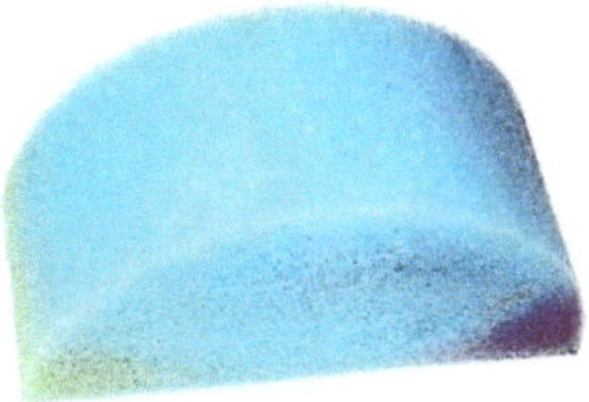

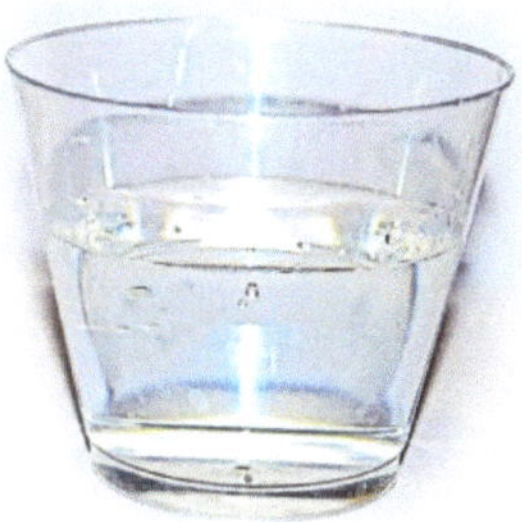

WATER-

FRESH, UNCONTAMINATED WATER SHOULD ALWAYS BE USED ON YOUR PAINT CAKES.

BRUSHES-

I PREFER TO KEEP MANY BRUSHES ON HAND, INCLUDING LONGER BRISTLES FOR OUTLINES, AND SHORTER BRISTLES FOR DOTS AND EMBELLISHMENTS.

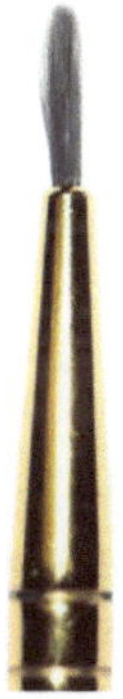

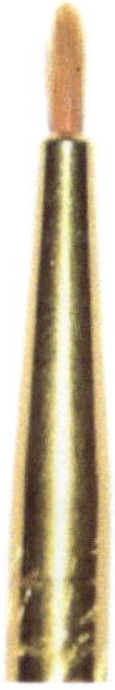

BUTTERFLY

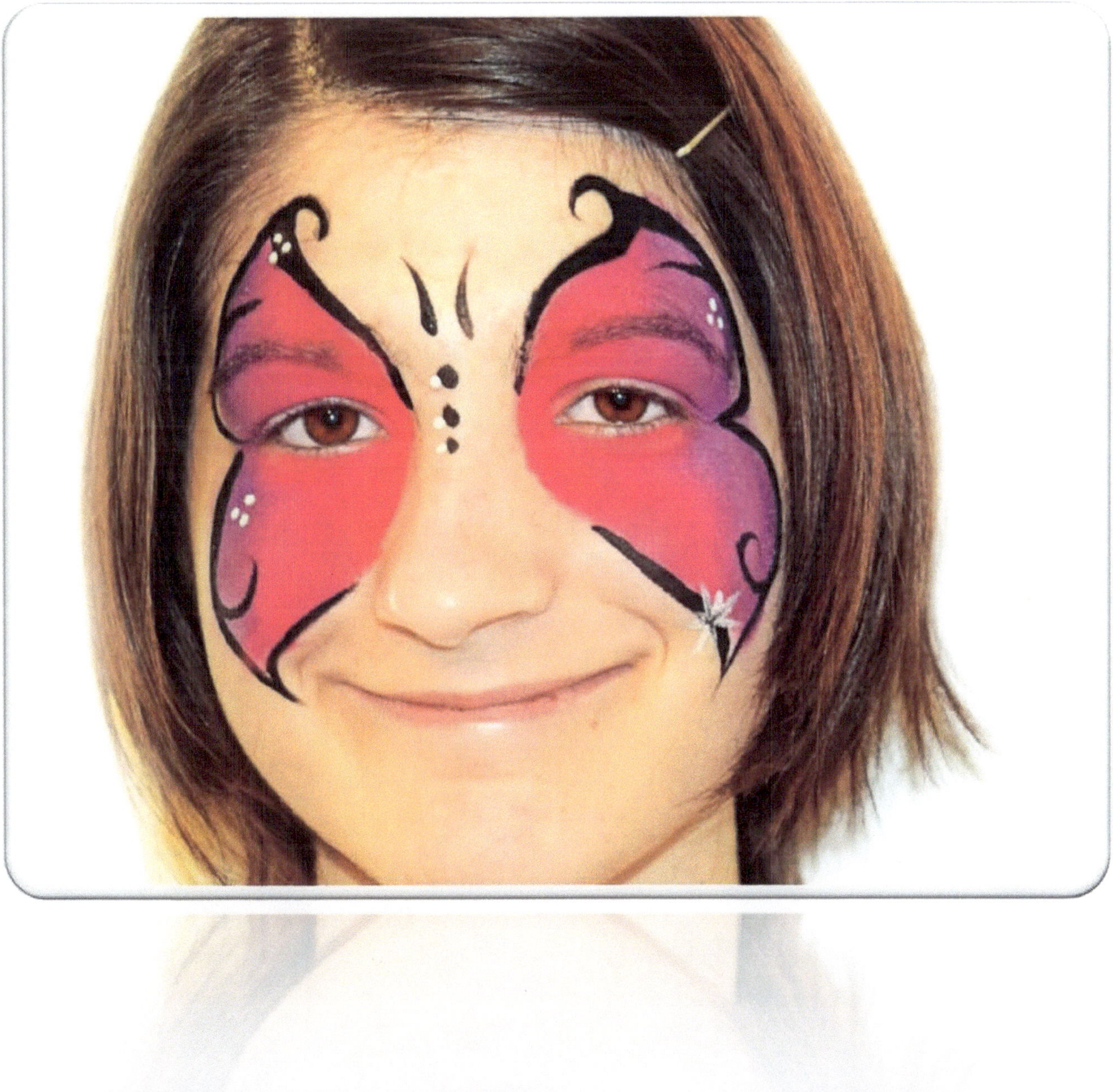

BUTTERFLY STEP-BY-STEP

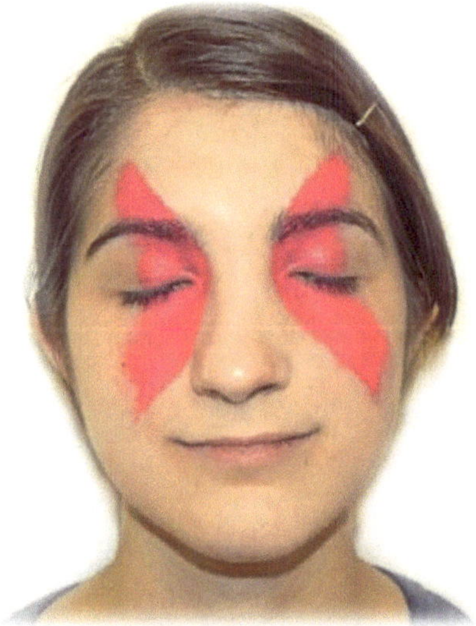

STEP 1 -

USING YOUR SPONGE, START FROM THE INNER EDGE OF THE EYE AND CREATE 'U' SHAPES OUTWARD TOWARDS THE EDGE OF THE FACE

STEP 2 -

WITH THE OTHER SIDE OF THE SPONGE AND A DIFFERENT COLOR, CREATE THE OPPOSITE 'U' SHAPE, WITH THE POINTS LEANING BACK TOWARDS THE ORIGINAL COLOR

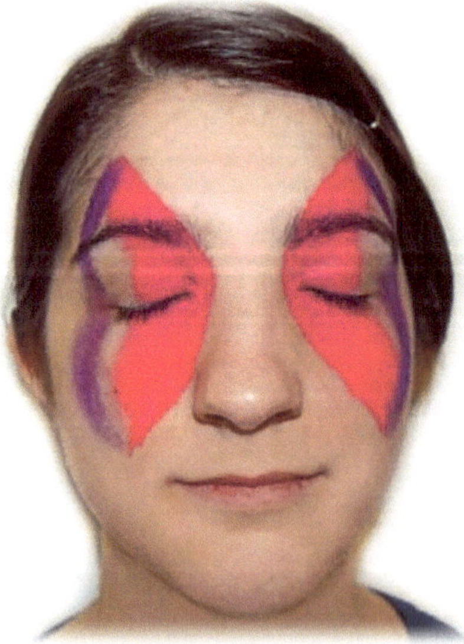

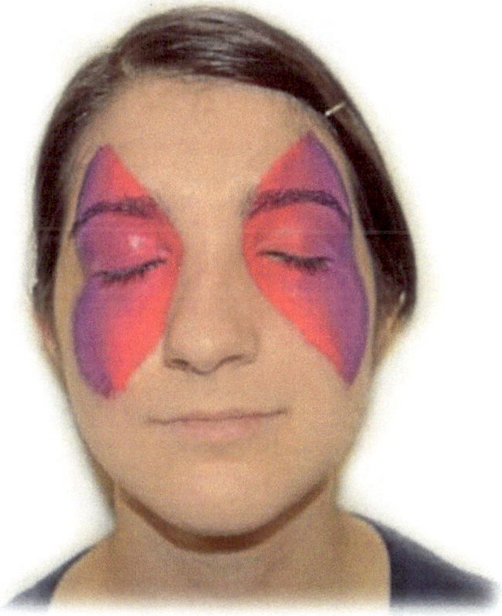

STEP 3 -

WORKING BACK AND FORTH BETWEEN THE TWO COLORS, BLEND THE TWO TOGETHER.

STEP 4 -

USING YOUR LONGER BRISTLED BRUSH, OUTLINE THE SHAPE OF YOUR BUTTERFLY, BRINGING THE TOP AND BOTTOM TIPS TO POINTS OR SWIRLS. THEN ADD ANTENNAS AND THREE DOTS FOR THE BODY, ALONG THE NOSE. YOU MAY ADDITIONALLY ADD WHITE DOTS AS ACCENTS.

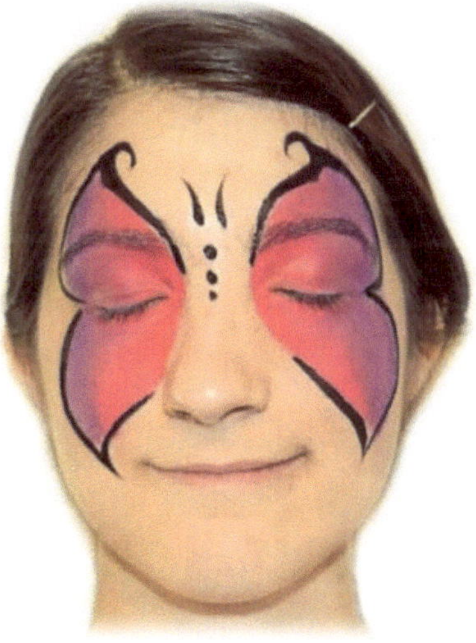

TIGER MASK

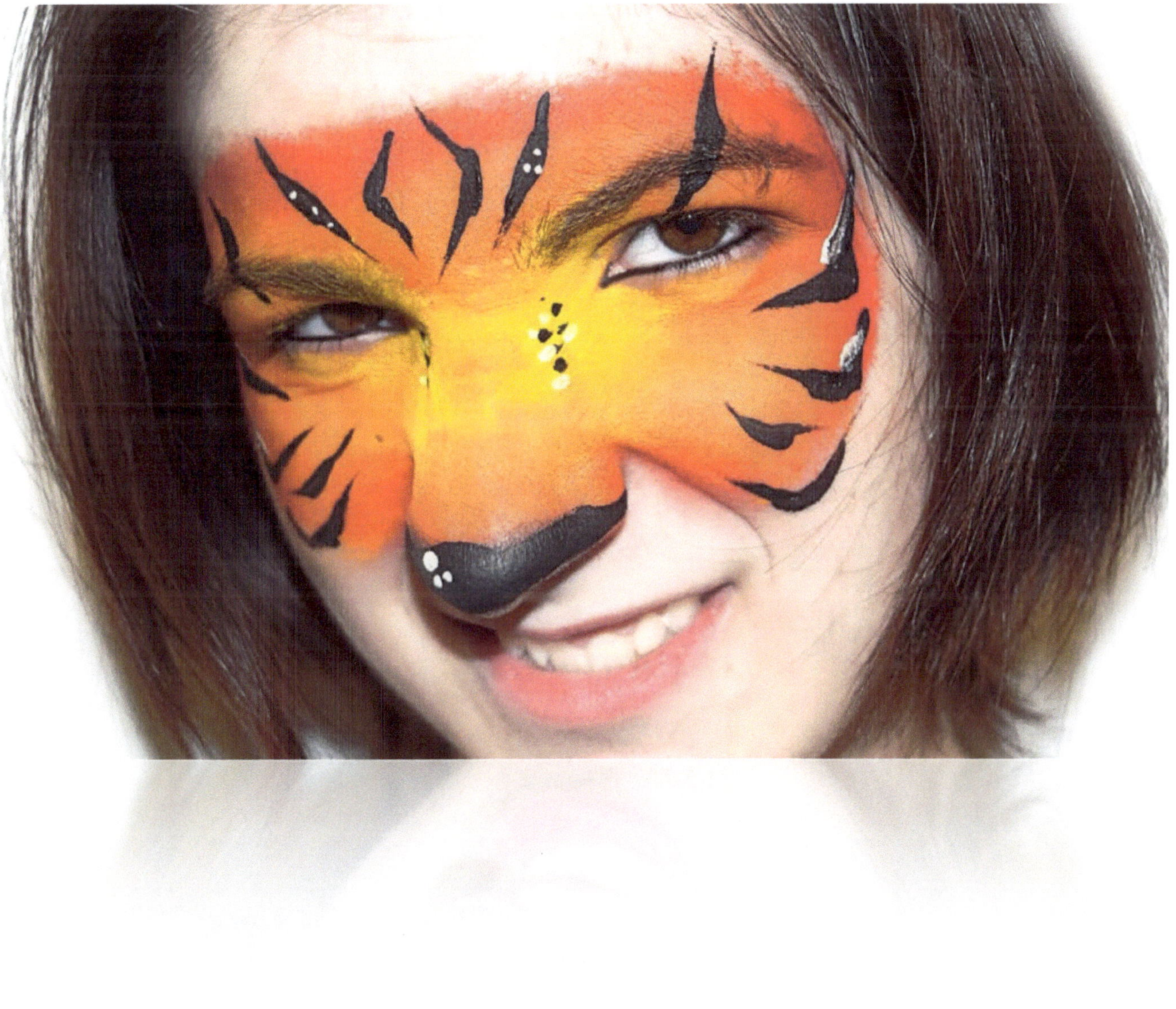

TIGER MASK STEP-BY-STEP

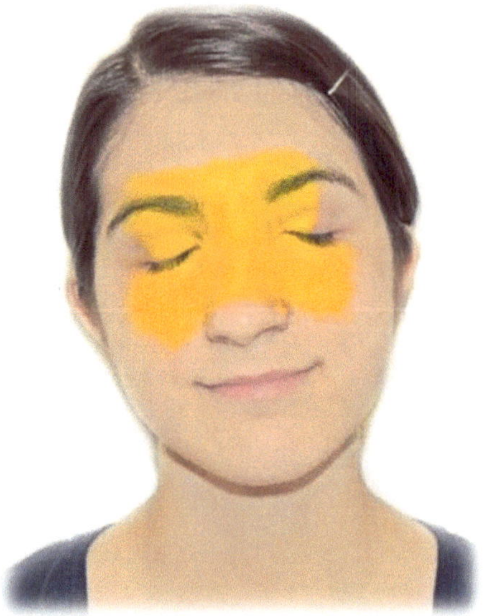

STEP 1 -

STARTING FROM THE CENTER OF THE NOSE AND USING YOUR SPONGE, CREATE A YELLOW CENTER THAT EXTENDS TO THE MIDDLE OF THE EYE AND JUST ABOVE THE EYEBROWS.

STEP 2 -

USING YOUR SPONGE AND ORANGE PAINT, CREATE THE OUTER SHAPE OF THE MASK AND BLEND THE TWO COLORS TOGETHER.

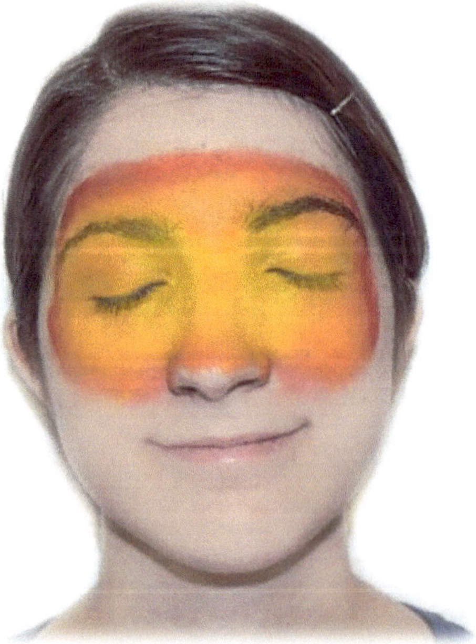

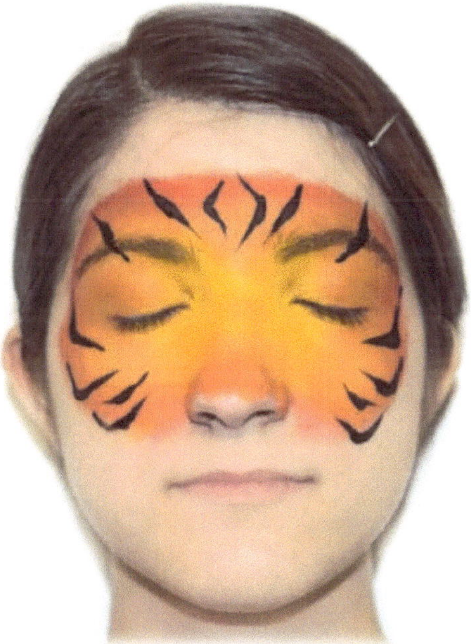

STEP 3 -

ADD TIGER STRIPES. ALL STRIPES SHOULD POINT TOWARDS THE CENTER OF THE NOSE. STRIPES ARE THIN (POINTED) ON THE ENDS, AND FAT IN THE MIDDLE. STRIPES ON THE SIDE CAN BE STRAIGHT, OR 'L' SHAPED TO FRAME THE MASK.

STEP 4 -

ADD DOTS TO THE SIDE OF THE NOSE NEAR THE EYE, AND PAINT THE TIP OF THE NOSE BLACK. YOU CAN ALSO ADD WHITE DOTS TO STRIPES AND NOSE.

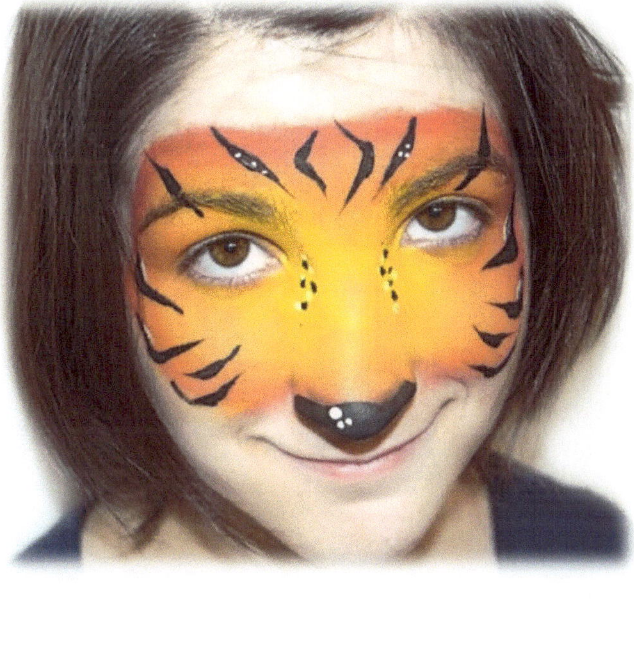

KITTY CAT

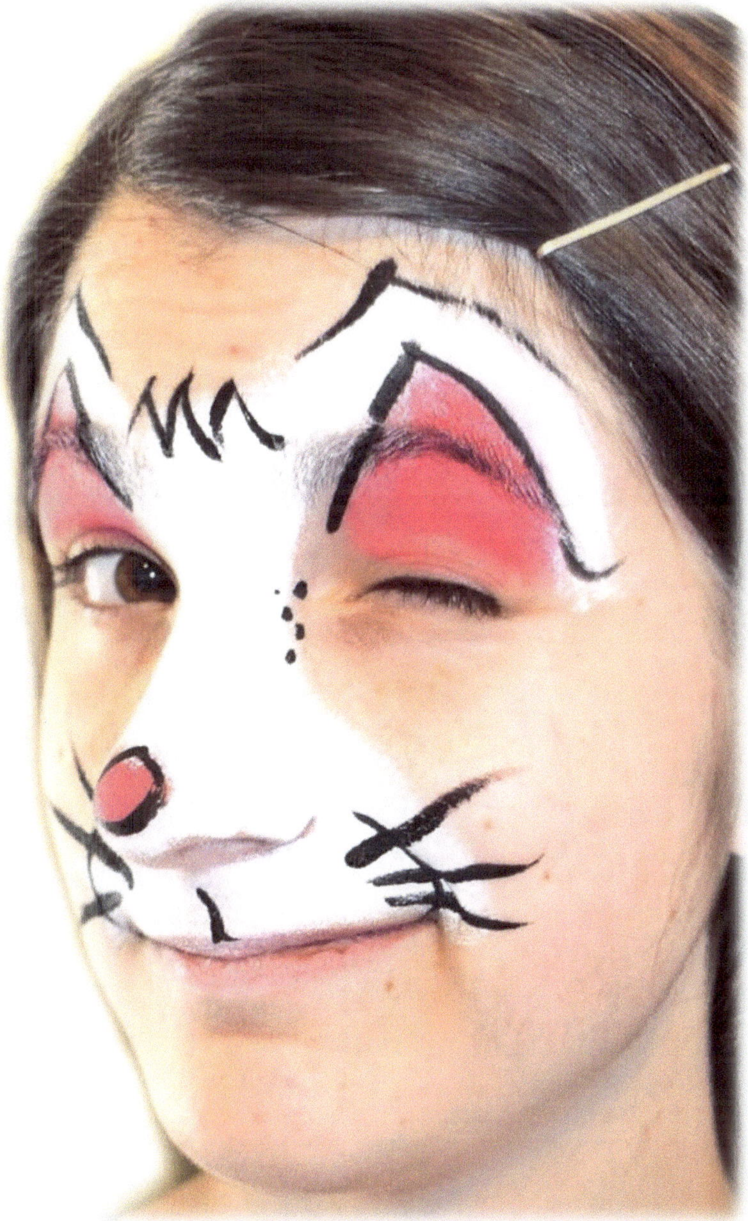

KITTY CAT STEP-BY-STEP

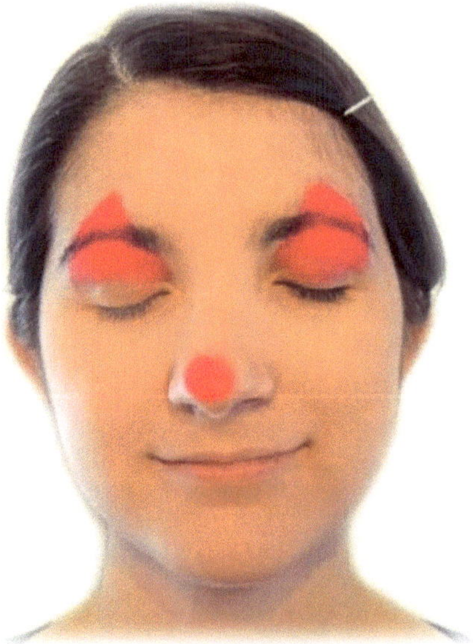

STEP 1 -

USING YOUR SPONGE OR BRUSH, PAINT PINK TRIANGLES OVER THE EYES, AND A PINK CIRCLE ON THE NOSE.

STEP 2 -

USING YOUR SPONGE, PAINT WHITE TRIANGLES OVER THE PINK ONES, THEN CONNECT THE TWO TRIANGLES AT THE BRIDGE OF THE NOSE. CONTINUE THE WHITE DOWN THE NOSE AND AROUND THE CIRCLE ON THE NOSE, THEN ADD THE 'MUZZLE' SHAPE BELOW THE NOSE AND ABOVE THE UPPER LIP.

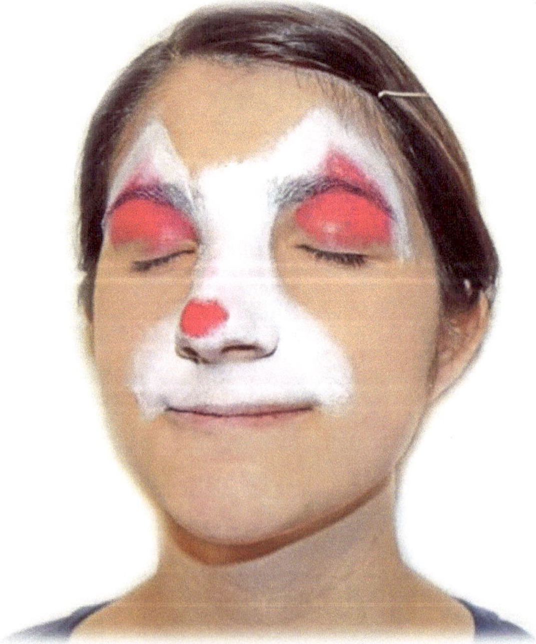

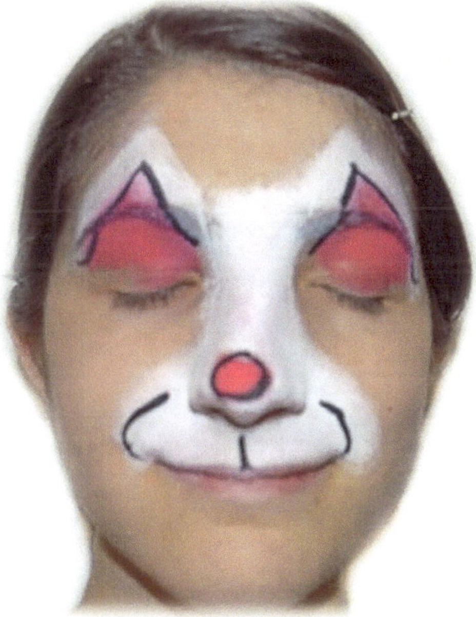

STEP 3 -

USING YOUR OUTLINING BRUSH, LOOSELY OUTLINE THE PINK TRIANGLES AND CIRCLE, AND THE MUZZLE SHAPE. ADD A LINE FROM THE BOTTOM OF THE NOSE TO THE TOP LIP.

STEP 4 -

ADD ANOTHER LOOSE OUTLINE TO THE TOP OF THE WHITE TRIANGLES, AND ADD SMALL BLACK TRIANGLES TO THE BRIDGE OF THE NOSE TO SIMULATE FUR. THEN FINISH THE OUTLINE BY ADDING WHISKERS EXTENDING FROM THE MUZZLE TOWARDS THE CHEEKS, AND ADD DOTS ALONGS THE SIDES OF THE NOSE.

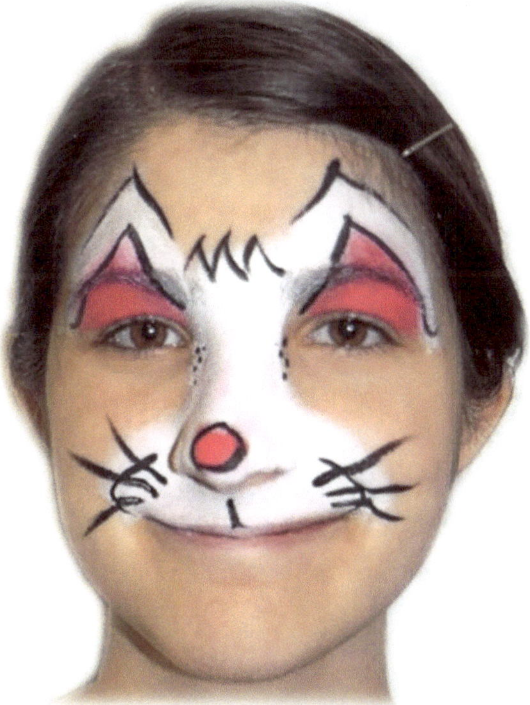

SCARY SKULL

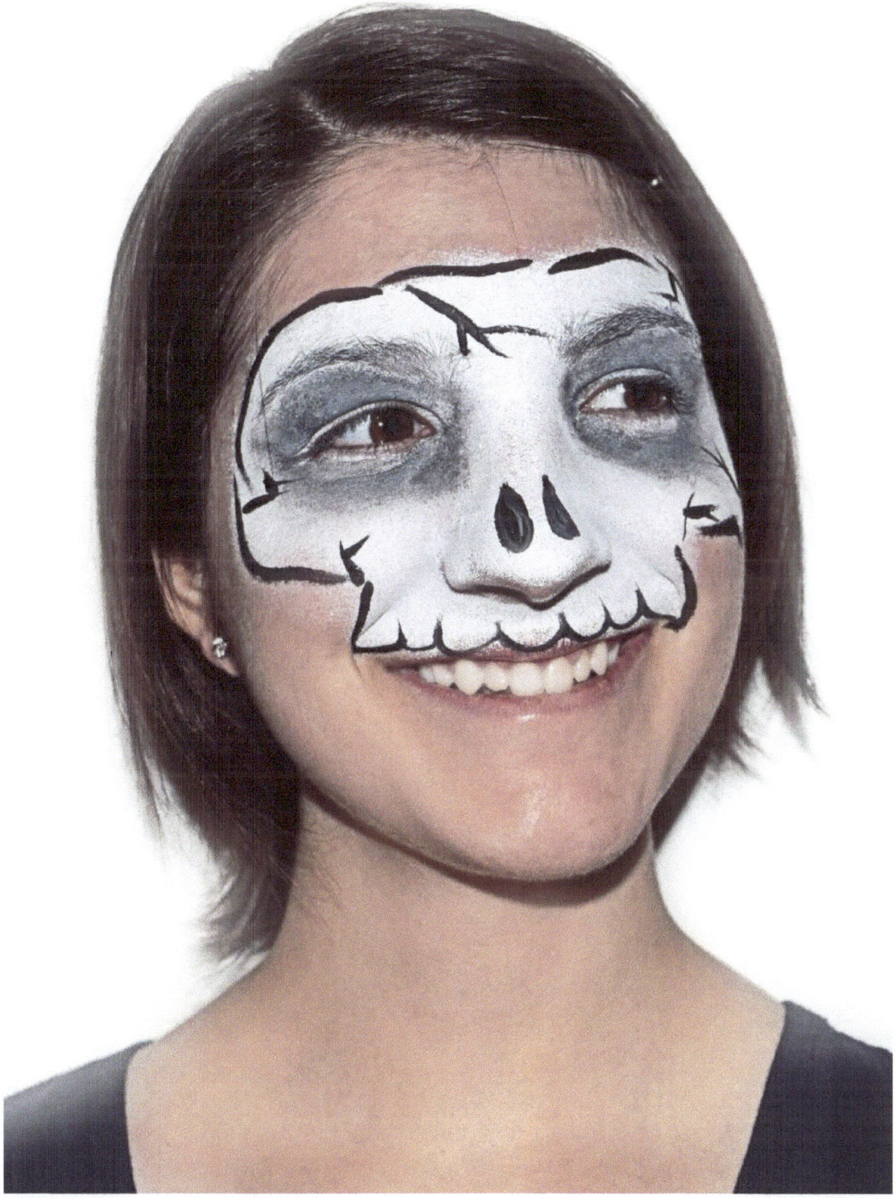

SCARY SKULL STEP-BY-STEP

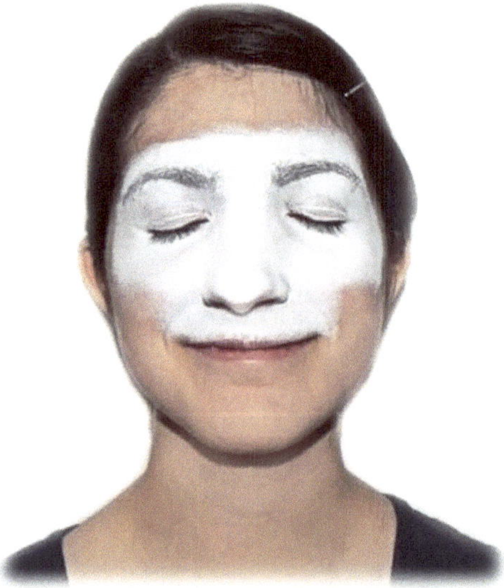

STEP 1 -

USING YOUR SPONGE, CREATE THE MASK SHAPE, LARGER OVER THE EYES AND SMALLER BETWEEN THE NOSE AND TOP LIP.

STEP 2 -

ADDING A BIT OF BLACK TO YOUR SPONGE, BLEND AND DARKEN THE AREA AROUND THE EYES.

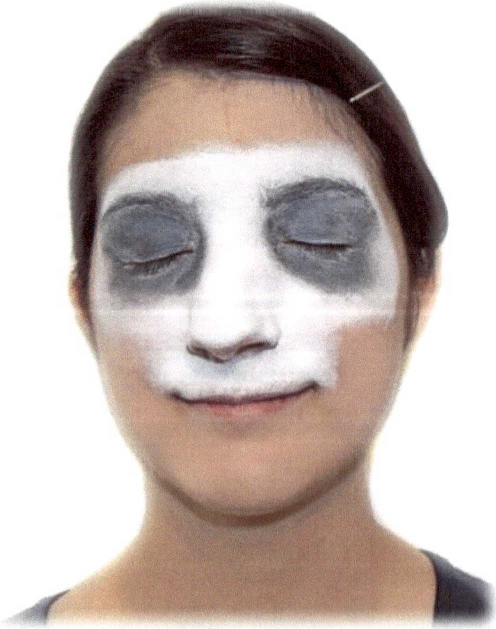

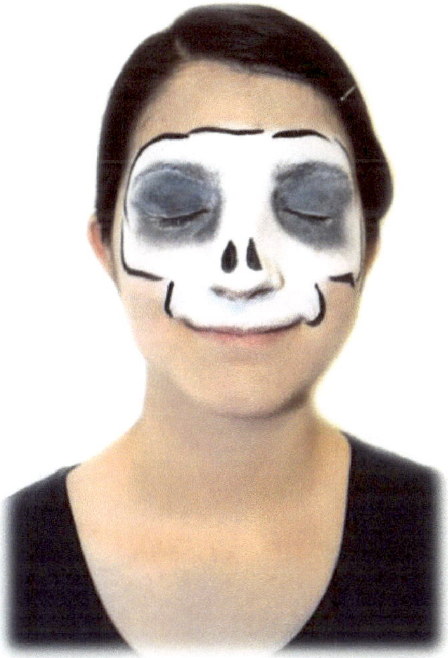

STEP 3 -

OUTLINE THE MASK SHAPE, AND ADD TWO LARGE ‘TEAR DROP’ SHAPES TO THE NOSE.

STEP 4 -

ADD CONNECTING ‘U’ SHAPES JUST ABOVE THE TOP LIP, AND ADD SMALL CONNECTING LINES OR ‘CRACKS’ EXTENDING INWARD FROM THE OUTER EDGE.

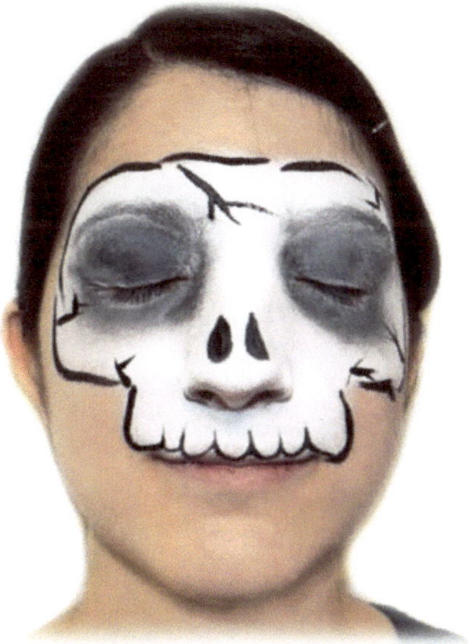

MONSTER MASK

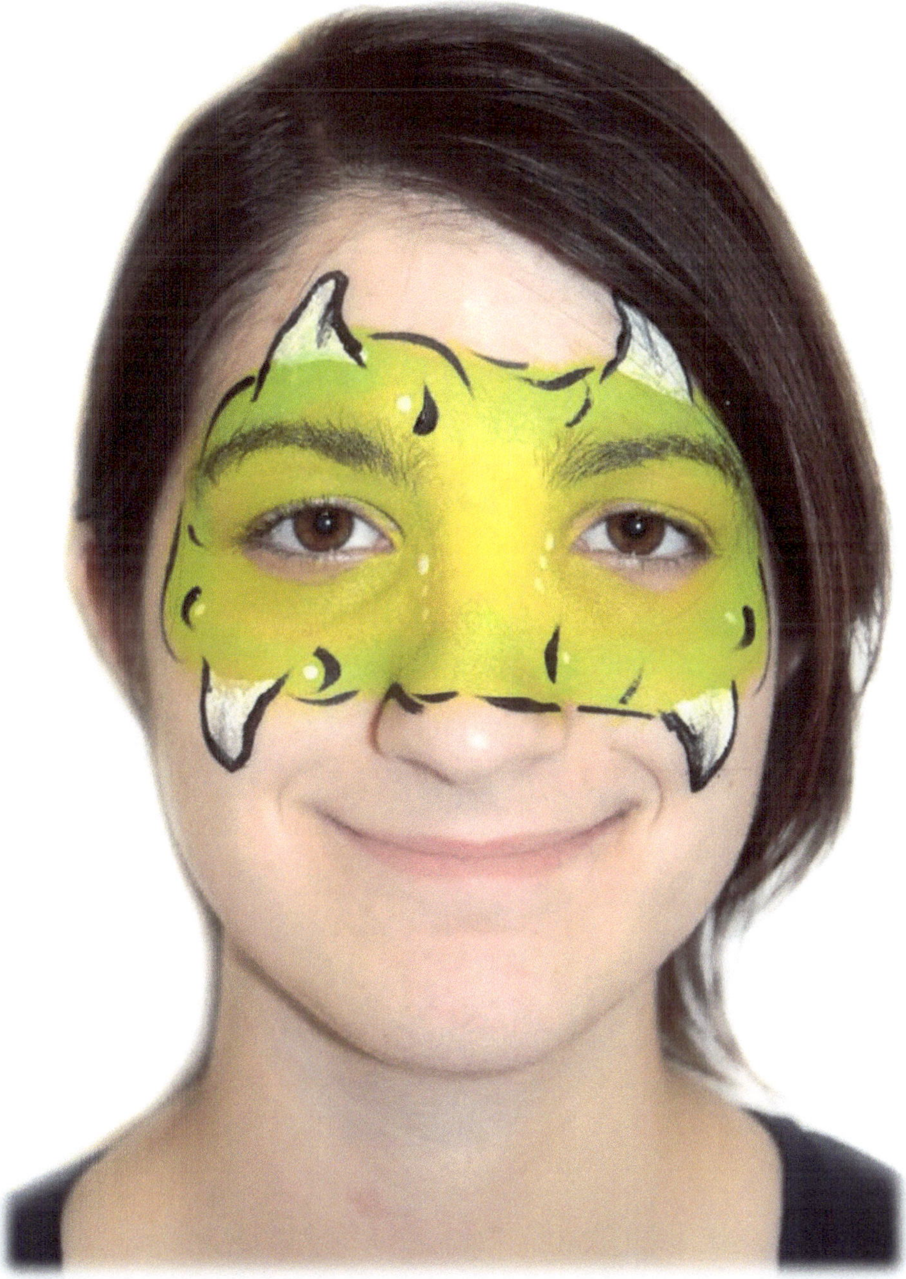

MONSTER MASK STEP-BY-STEP

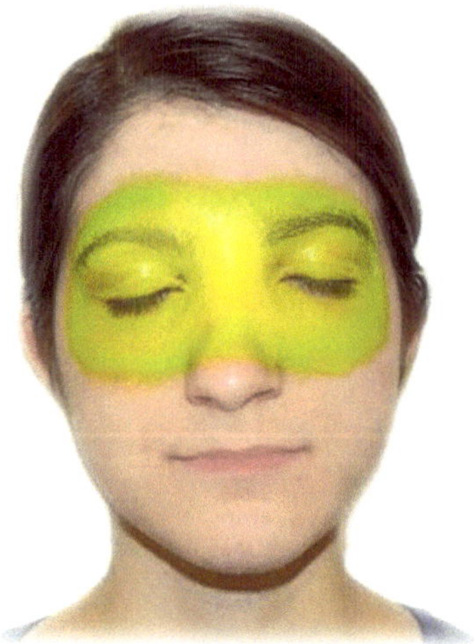

STEP 1 -

LOAD YOUR SPONGE WITH BOTH GREEN AND YELLOW PAINT, AND CREATE THE MASK SHAPE, KEEPING THE YELLOW TOWARD THE INSIDE OF THE MASK.

STEP 2 -

USING YOUR BRUSH, ADD FOUR 'HORNS', TWO ON THE TOP AND TWO ON THE BOTTOM. USE POINTED HORNS FOR OLDER FACES, AND BLUNTED HORNS FOR YOUNGER FACES.

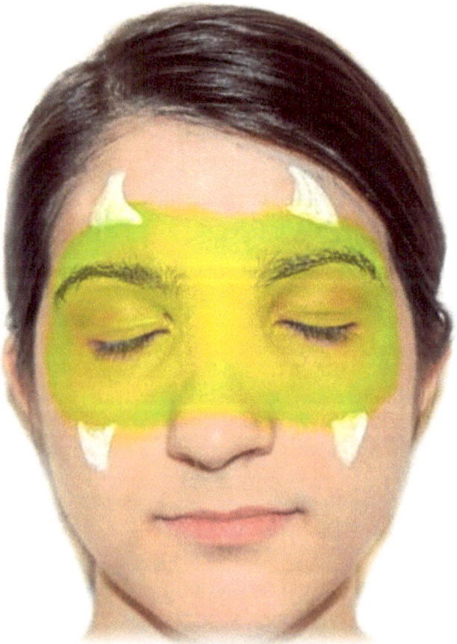

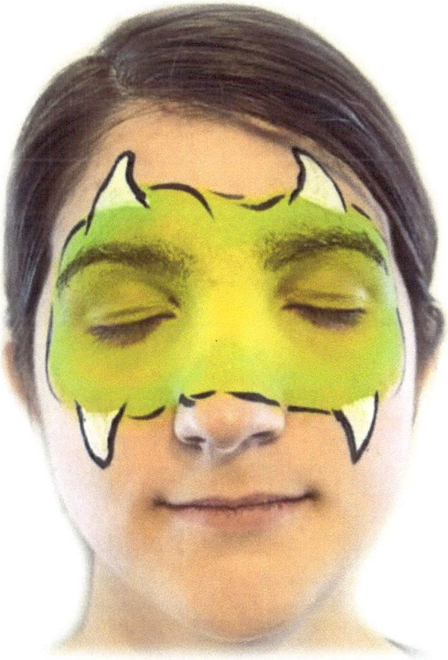

STEP 3 -

OUTLINE THE EDGES OF THE MASK AND THE HORNS. LINES THAT OUTLINE HORNS SHOULD BE EXTENDED SLIGHTLY INTO THE CENTER OF THE MASK.

STEP 4 -

ADD APOSTROPHY SHAPES INSIDE THE MASK, AND FINISH WITH A SINGLE WHITE DOT ON THE INSIDE OF EACH APOSTROPHY SHAPE.

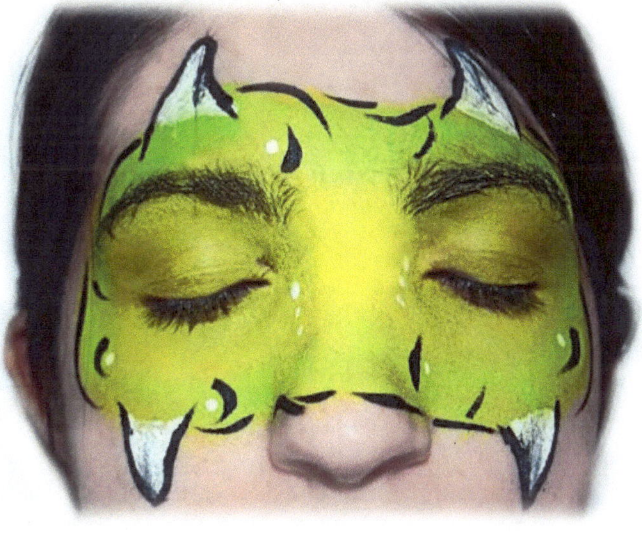

CHRISTEN HARRIS HAS BEEN A PROFESSIONAL FACE PAINTER SINCE 2008. SHE RESIDES IN PASCO COUNTY, FLORIDA WITH HER HUSBAND AND CHILDREN.

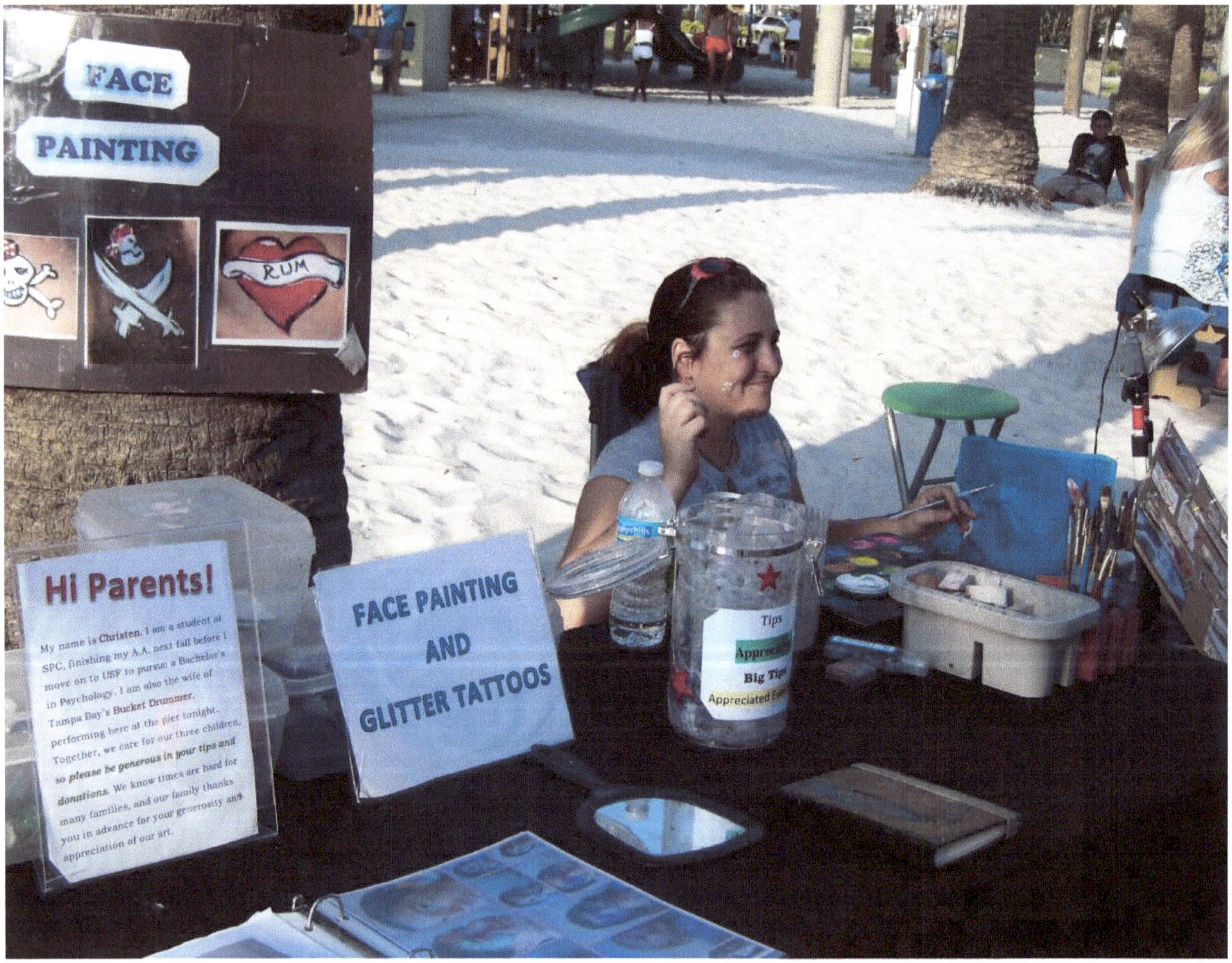

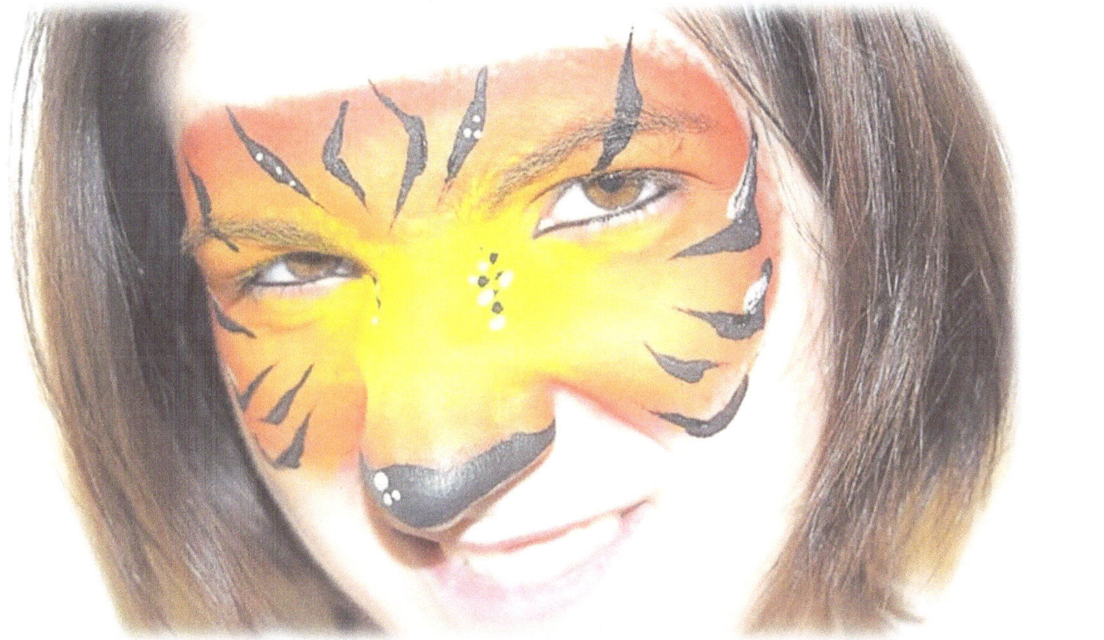

THANK YOU FOR PURCHASING THIS BOOK, AND FOR KEEPING THE ART OF FACE PAINTING ALIVE.
KEEP AN EYE OUT IN THE FUTURE FOR THE NEXT BOOK IN THIS SERIES:

FACE PAINTING
GO!
Book 2: INTERMEDIATE DESIGNS

www.ingramcontent.com/pod-product-compliance
Lightning Source LLC
Chambersburg PA
CBHW050414180526
45159CB00005B/2276
9781530117130